Made possible through the support of the University
of Nebraska Press with the Offices of the Chancellor
and Vice Chancellor for Research

University of Nebraska Press ♥ Lincoln & London

VALENTINES

VALENTINES

Ted Kooser

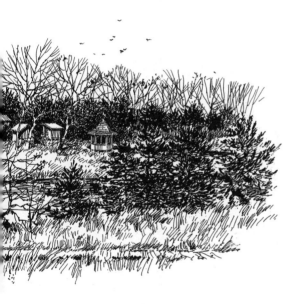

With an introduction by the poet

Illustrated by Robert Hanna

Acknowledgment for the use of
previously published material
appears on p. 47, which constitutes
an extension of the copyright page.

Publication of this book was
made possible by the generous
support of the University of
Nebraska Foundation.

LIBRARY OF CONGRESS
Cataloging-in-Publication Data
Kooser, Ted.
   Valentines / Ted Kooser ; with
a new introduction by the poet ;
Illustrated by Robert Hanna.
                p.   cm.
ISBN-13: 978-0-8032-1770-6
                   (cloth : alk. paper)
ISBN-10: 0-8032-1770-6
                   (cloth : alk. paper)
   1. Valentine's Day—Poetry.
I. Title.
                PS3561.O6V35 2008
811'.54—dc22   2007036548

Designed and set in
Monotype Dante by A. Shahan.

To the memory of Laura Casari

Early in 1986 I stole the idea of sending out an annual valentine from our longtime family friend, Dace Burdic, who had been making and sending her own valentines for a number of years. Dace is a woman who enjoys having fun, and I'm pretty sure she'd agree that there's never quite enough fun for any of us. So I'd guess she doesn't mind that I've hitched my coal car to her locomotive. But let's say "coal *tender*" instead, since we're talking about valentines.

That first year I wrote "Pocket Poem," which you'll find here, and sent it to about fifty women, many of them the wives of my friends. My wife, Kathleen, didn't seem to mind, and she's tolerated this foolishness of mine every year since, as the list grew and grew. She's not only a good sport; she also knows that though I'm a flirt, I'm pretty much a harmless geezer much like the one in that wonderful John Crowe Ransom poem, "Piazza Piece," which begins with an old man addressing a group of young women:

> I am a gentleman in a dustcoat trying
> To make you hear. Your ears are soft and small
> And listen to an old man not at all,
> They want the young men's whispering and sighing . . .

My valentines were printed on standard-sized postcards, which saved a lot on the ever-rising first-class postage, and in the years when I got them written and printed in time I'd send them up to Valentine, Nebraska, to be postmarked from there. Over the past several years, during which I've done a lot of poetry readings around the country, I'd ask for the names and mailing addresses of women in the audience who might like to be on my valentine list. By the 2007 Valentine's Day mailing I had around twenty-six hundred names of women on the list, and the printing and stamps ran into hundreds of dollars. So I put a note on the 2007 card saying that this one would be the last. But for this book I've included one last valentine, for 2008. I wrote it for Kathleen, and it's only fitting that my last annual valentine poem should turn its attention back to her. You'll see that this last poem is indeed the poem of a man who has careened beyond the romantic into an altogether different age.

I hope you have fun with these poems. I suppose some of them have a little literary merit but, really, they were written with pleasure and meant for the reader's fun. I hope you enjoy the reading half as much as I enjoyed the writing, the licking of stamps, and the addressing to all those women who were willing to tolerate my foolishness.

ILLUSTRATOR'S NOTE

Robert Hanna

The illustrations created to accompany the poems in this book are not meant to represent the poems themselves, but rather give a glimpse of the world where they were written. The art is meant to reflect the aesthetic temper of Ted's writing space—which includes his home, his work shed, and the rolling landscape of Nebraska's Bohemian Alps—and reveal the heartland that provides his inspiration.

VALENTINES

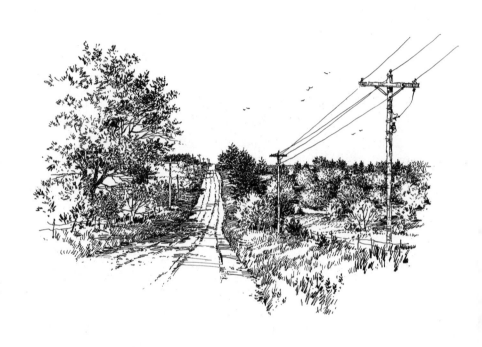

POCKET POEM

If this comes creased and creased again and soiled
as if I'd opened it a thousand times
to see if what I'd written here was right,
it's all because I looked too long for you
to put it in your pocket. Midnight says
the little gifts of loneliness come wrapped
by nervous fingers. What I wanted this
to say was that I want to be so close
that when you find it, it is warm from me.

A PERFECT HEART

To make a perfect heart you take a sheet
of red construction paper of the type
that's rough as a cat's tongue, fold it once,
and crease it really hard, so it feels
as if your thumb might light up like a match,

then choose your scissors from the box. I like
those safety scissors with the sticky blades
and the rubber grips that pinch a little skin
as you snip along. They make you careful,
just as you should be, cutting out a heart

for someone you love. Don't worry that your curve
won't make a valentine; it will. Rely
on chewing on your lip and symmetry
to guide your hand along with special art.
And there it is at last: a heart, a heart!

CHOCOLATE CHECKERS

In a tiny green park, chopped out
of a corner of Commerce, I saw
two men in rags with their backpacks
lying beside them. Red nose to red nose
and old boots toe to toe, they were
playing a game of chocolate checkers,
using candy for pieces, and eating
the pieces they'd won from each other
and laughing like crazy.

                      It was Commerce
who'd given this park to the city,
and Commerce looked on — the bank
and the telephone company
standing behind mirrored windows,
disapproving — not of chocolate checkers,
per se, but of that kind of people,
laughing and playing with candy
on an imported Italian marble table
with neatly set black-and-white tiles.

A HEART OF GOLD

It's an old beer bottle
with a heart of gold. There's a lot
of defeat in those shoulders,
sprinkled with dandruff, battered
by years of huddling up
with good buddies, out of the wind.

This is no throwaway bottle.
Full of regret and sad stories,
here it comes, back into your life
again and again, ready to stand
in front of everyone you know
and let you peel its label off.

Now, from the wet formica tabletop,
it lifts its sweet old mouth to yours.

HOME STORAGE BARNS

They're easy to see from the freeway,
backed into fences like cattle
and showing their ribs to the wind,
or standing up under the eaves
of a house, holding a dog on a chain—

little red valentine barns in which
scholarly spiders relax in their carrels,
having related one thing to another,
one year to the next, having tied all
the loose ends. Or there are those

unsold and still empty as barrels,
by the dozens in lumberyard lots,
waiting for someone who's wanted
a barn all his life that will fit
a small place in the present,

a barn of a reasonable scale,
yet that looks like a barn ought to look
to a person who's dreaming
(with an X of white boards on the door
as if making a spot for the heart).

BARN OWL

High in the chaffy, taffy-colored haze
of the hayloft, up under the starry
nail-hole twinkle of the old tin roof,
there in a nest of straw and baling twine
I have hidden my valentine for you:
a white heart woven of snowy feathers
in which wide eyes of welcome open
to you as you climb the rickety ladder
into my love. Behind those eyes lies
a boudoir of intimate darkness, darling,
the silks of oblivion. And set like a jewel
dead center in the heart is a golden hook
the size of a finger ring, to hold you
always, plumpest sweetheart mouse of mine.

SONG OF THE IRONING BOARD

So many hands lay hot on my belly
over the years, and oh, how many ghosts
I held, their bodies damp and slack,
their long arms fallen to either side.
I gave till my legs shook, but then
they were up and away. Thus the lovely
soft nap of my youth was worn down.
But I gave of myself and was proud.

I was there for those Saturday
touch-ups, those solemn Sunday
sacraments of Clorox in the church
of starch, the hangers ringing.
On stiffening legs I suffered
the steam iron's hot incontinence,
the melt-down of the rayon slacks,
my batting going varicose.

And it all came down to this:
a cellar window looking out
on February, where a cold wind
pinches clothespins down an empty line.
I lean against the wall and breathe
the drifting smoke of memory,
a stained chemise pulled over
my scorched yet ever shining heart.

IN A LIGHT LATE-WINTER WIND

In a light late-winter wind
the oak trees are scattering valentines
over the snow—dark red
like the deep-running, veinous blood
of the married, returning
again and again to the steady heart.

This leaf is yours, friend,
picked from the heart-shaped hoofprint
of a deer. She stood here
under the apple tree during the night,
kicking up sweetness, her great eyes
watching the sleeping house.

THE CELERY HEART

CELERY HEARTS: 98 CENTS
—*Placard at Hinky Dinky*

Surely it misses those long fly balls of light
its leaves once leapt to catch, or longs to run
its roots out into the salty darkness.

What once looked like a Roman fountain
is now a ruin of fallen columns
bedded on ice. Its only consolations are,

at regular intervals, the hiss of mist,
and at times the warm and reassuring squeeze
of passing hand. But better this, by far,

than to be the sullen heart of artichoke,
stripped of its knives and heavy armor
and mummified for eons in a jar of brine.

FOR YOU, FRIEND,

this Valentine's Day, I intend to stand
for as long as I can on a kitchen stool
and hold back the hands of the clock,
so that wherever you are, you may walk
even more lightly in your loveliness;
so that the weak, mid-February sun
(whose chill I will feel from the face
of the clock) cannot in any way
lessen the lights in your hair, and the wind
(whose subtle insistence I will feel
in the minute hand) cannot tighten
the corners of your smile. People
drearily walking the winter streets
will long remember this day:
how they glanced up to see you
there in a storefront window, glorious,
strolling along on the outside of time.

IN THE ALLEY

In the alley behind the florist's shop,
a huge white garbage truck was parked and idling.
In a cloud of exhaust, two men in coveralls
and stocking caps, their noses dripping,
were picking through the florist's dumpster
and each had selected a fistful of roses.

As I walked past, they gave me a furtive,
conspiratorial nod, perhaps sensing
that I, too (though in my business suit and tie)
am a devotee of garbage—an aficionado
of the wilted, the shopworn, and the free—
and that I had for days been searching
beneath the heaps of worn-out, faded words
to find this brief bouquet for you.

TRACKS

Using a cobbler's shoe last
I found one summer at a yard sale,
and the heavy leather uppers
from cast-off boots, a jigsaw,
some wood, an awl and thread,
and a few evenings sitting alone
thinking of you, I have fashioned
a pair of red valentine shoes
with heart-shaped wooden heels.
Look for my tracks on your doorstep
where I stood with sore feet
through the evening, too timid to knock.

THE BLUET

Of all the flowers, the bluet has
the sweetest name, two syllables
that form on the lips, then fall
with a tiny, raindrop splash
into a suddenly bluer morning.

I offer you mornings like that,
fragrant with tiny blue blossoms —
each with four petals, each with a star
at its heart. I would give you whole fields
of wild perfume if only

you could be mine, if you were not —
like the foolish bluet (also called
Innocence) — always holding your face
to the fickle, careless, fly-by kiss
of the Clouded Sulphur Butterfly.

IF YOU FEEL SORRY

If you feel sorry for yourself
this Valentine's Day, think of
the dozens of little paper poppies
left in the box when the last
of the candy is gone, how *they*
must feel, dried out and brown
in their sad old heart-shaped box,
without so much as a single finger
to scrabble around in their
crinkled petals, not even
one pimpled nose to root and snort
through their delicate pot pourri.
So before you make too much
of being neglected, I want you
to think how *they* feel.

A MAP OF THE WORLD

One of the ancient maps of the world
is heart-shaped, carefully drawn
and once washed with bright colors,
though the colors have faded
as you might expect feelings to fade
from a fragile old heart, the brown map
of a life. But feeling is indelible,
and longing infinite, a starburst compass
pointing in all the directions
two lovers might go, a fresh breeze
swelling their sails, the future uncharted,
still far from the edge
where the sea pours into the stars.

INVENTORY

How gentle she is with the boxes of candy hearts,
as with one finger she deftly tips the front rack forward
and breathes in the talcummy odor of those behind
who eagerly whisper LOVER, KISS ME, and BE MINE
in sugary voices. They cannot see her free hand,
hidden below the shelf, which with unsentimental fingers
swiftly tallies their type and price and number
on a black machine that hangs from her neck on a strap.
Then, with no word of farewell, she moves away
and begins to tweak and pinch and jostle the bags
of chocolate kisses, to gently punch the gummy bears,
her hidden hand tapping the while. Then, without so much
as a wink of warning, she suddenly shoves her whole arm,
naked but for a friendship bracelet, into their rustle
and begins feeling around. I stick out my old man's chest,
throw back my pigeon shoulders, and tremble a little
as, unnoticed and uncounted, I push my cart past.

SKATER

She was all in black but for a yellow pony tail
that trailed from her cap, and bright blue gloves
that she held out wide, the feathery fingers spread,
as surely she stepped, click-clack, onto the frozen
top of the world. And there, with a clatter of blades,
she began to braid a loose path that broadened
into a meadow of curls. Across the ice she swooped
and then turned back and, halfway, bent her legs
and leapt into the air the way a crane leaps, blue gloves
lifting her lightly, and turned a snappy half-turn
there in the wind before coming down, arms wide,
skating backward right out of that moment, smiling back
at the woman she'd been just an instant before.

SCREECH OWL

All night each reedy whinny
from a bird no bigger than a heart
flies out of a tall black pine
and, in a breath, is taken away
by the stars. Yet, with small hope
from the center of darkness
it calls out again and again.

SPLITTING AN ORDER

I like to watch an old man cutting a sandwich in half,
maybe an ordinary cold roast beef on whole wheat bread,
no pickles or onion, keeping his shaky hands steady
by placing his forearms firm on the edge of the table
and using both hands, the left to hold the sandwich in place,
and the right to cut it surely, corner to corner,
observing his progress through glasses that moments before
he wiped with his napkin, and then to see him lift half
onto the extra plate that he had asked the server to bring,
and then to wait, offering the plate to his wife
while she slowly unrolls her napkin and places her spoon,
her knife and her fork in their proper places,
then smoothes the starched white napkin over her knees
and meets his eyes and holds out both old hands to him.

A NEW POTATO

This is just one of the leathery eggs
the scuffed-up, dirty turtle of the moon
buried early in spring, her eyes like stars
fixed on the future, and, inside its red skin,
whiteness, like all of the moons to come,
and marvelous, buttered with light.

OH, MARIACHI ME

All my life I have wanted nothing so much
as the love of women. For them I have fashioned
the myth of myself, the singing troubadour
with the flashing eyes. Always for them
my black sombrero with its swinging tassels,
this vest embroidered with hearts, these trousers
with silver studs down the seams. Oh, I am
Mariachi me, as I had intended. I am success
and the price of success, now old and dusty
at the edge of the dance floor, still smiling,
heavy with hope, clutching my dead guitar.

THIS PAPER BOAT

Carefully placed upon the future,
it tips from the breeze and skims away,
frail thing of words, this valentine,
so far to sail. And if you find it
caught in the reeds, its message blurred,
the thought that you are holding it
a moment is enough for me.

THE HOG-NOSED SNAKE

The hog-nosed snake, when playing dead,
Lets its tongue loll out of its ugly head.

It lies on its back as stiff as a stick;
If you flip it over it'll flip back quick.

If I seem dead when you awake,
Just flip me once, like the hog-nosed snake.